**Poems of a
Palestinian
Boyhood**

Poems of a Palestinian Boyhood
Reja-e Busailah

STACK BOOKS

Smokestack Books
1 Lake Terrace, Grewelthorpe, Ripon HG4 3BU
e-mail: info@smokestack-books.co.uk
www.smokestack-books.co.uk

ISBN 9781916012134

Smokestack Books
is represented
by Inpress Ltd

for my people

Contents

Preface

The poems in this volume have been written over many years under various circumstances, personal and general, hence their variety of styles. I have not written them for any reason other than to write them in reaction to various experiences, some new, others recollected. The idea of putting them in a volume came to me only while I was writing a memoir dealing with the fifteen years or so of my life when I was a child during the period 1932-1948, *In the Land of My Birth: A Palestinian Boyhood* (published in 2017 by the Institute for Palestine Studies). Thus, if the memoir makes up the pictures or the scenes, these poems are reflections on the same events. It is difficult to tell which of the two (the poems or the memoir) has primacy. It is safer to assert that they feed each other. The poems are a commentary on, or reaction to, events and circumstances related to this period in the life of the author. They are glimpses, as it were, into his life during this period. At first I wanted to include them within the memoir since they are all related directly or indirectly to the period above mentioned. But I soon realized that this was impracticable when I discovered that there were too many poems which qualified to be included. Though the poems record the experiences of a child growing into boyhood, blind from infancy, they are by no means intended as mere comments on specific events – history, geography, psychology, sociology, not even autobiography. Of course, they do refer to many of these, but they remain first and foremost poems, each written for its own sake, each independent from one another.

I have lived in the West for over fifty years, but I spent my formative years in the East. Every poem is thus a product of this duality. There is much of the West in every poem, but there is perhaps more of the East, especially of the land of my birth, Palestine. It goes without saying that the arrangement of the poems into divisions creates overlapping. After all, poetry recognizes no borders. A poem may legitimately juxtapose a number of themes sometimes similar, sometimes contradictory. Moods and themes echo each other from all the divisions. They do so with various degrees and in various ways. Sometimes the connection is direct, sometimes oblique, and sometimes quite slight.

The order in which the poems have been arranged is not to signify a division in theme or subject. They do not allow for this. Rather, they have been arranged in this way in order to signify, with the exception of the fourth division, merely a shift in emphasis.

Thus, selecting a poem to signify the general theme and tone for the section is more symbolic than anything else. In the first section, 'The Time It Was' attempts to give a picture of what life was before the climax, a sense of when tranquility and security prevailed. The poems introduced by 'The Spider' say much about the education of the child and his emancipation from the restrictions of blindness in particular and childhood in general. In the last section, life goes on, but primarily as the speaker sees it, a sort of reconciliation and a hint of hope. Life continues, so does the struggle.

The first section is concerned with the child, with his limited experience, with nothing yet to presage or hint at what is awaiting him and his country. Most of them express childhood which is complacent or satisfactory though some deal with the child's unhappiness or inconvenience. Like the poems in other sections, the poems here refer fully or in part to their initial place or scene of origin, to one or more places the child lived in or visited in his country.

In the second part, it is the subject which determines the arrangement of the poems. They all deal with questions relating to religion in one way or another. They cover a wider range in the life of the child – from the time he started memorizing the Qur'an under the supervision of his father through his schooling at the house for orphans, and then the 'Alaiyyah School until his reconciliation with his religion and his encounters with Christianity. It must be noted that the child's experiences here are far from being adequately represented by the poems. But adequate representation was not in the author's mind when composing the poems.

In the third part the poems share a special and important characteristic. This is the obsession of the boy with the doings of the British occupiers and Zionist invaders of the country. Their presence constitutes a real and graphic menace. We stand, as it were, on the brink. Some of the poems deal directly and some indirectly with the boy's worryings and fears. He half-knows that something bad is going to happen or even about to happen. It spoils things for him and his friends. It intrudes on their innocent pleasures.

The fourth part deals primarily with the process of the conquest of the country and the physical uprooting of its people – from the skirmishing with the British, through the great rebellion (1936-1939) against the British and the Zionist Jews, to the climax of 1948. The poems here attempt to represent various aspects of this experience, from the specific or general to the anecdotal.

These poems in the fifth section strike a less somber note. Some offer commentaries, others explanations while others directly express optimism, the will and determination to win. 'Journey of a Curse' has been included here since it ends affirming the triumph over the predicament of blindness, thus also symbolizing the triumph of justice over injustice.

Reja-e Busailah
Kokomo, Indiana
2019

I

The Time it Was

It is hard to tell the time it was:
when cherry and apricot attained full knowledge
and threw it in rapture
to wind and growing sun;

when apple and pear quit at last
and left in reflective sun
dark grape to contemplate flight;

or when cats still watched their shadows
lengthening before ripening
into dreams of rough play with afternoon heat –
hard to tell, yet we know full well it was there:

in the mood of endless sky
when the moment falls off track
and all goes swimming out of time and place,
and every shadow is about to breathe
its last in the other
and none doing so,
for fear of breaking the spell,
of knowing and thereby becoming
the finite.

A Cluster

A luxuriant cluster of children
frisking and frolicking near August's end
on the broad ledge of light
starting to go obsolete,

in the honeysuckled excitement
echoing in the folds of the sky
ribs nudging ribs
scoffing at the gathering gloam,

eyeballs looking like cherries
impatient on the threshold of puberty
and lustrous voices swelling
tangling with the remnants of the sun –

still cleaner than the bosoms of nuns.

The Ides of March

I was peeling an orange to eat
on the Ides of March;
it bore the bright gold of a steep sunset;
my thought fell way back into the month of December,
the month when the year is precipitously buried,

when the orange hits puberty
grouching and growling,
as is the custom of puberty these days,
the peel was recalcitrant
squirting angry oil all over;

it was such labour to uncloak the fruit
as made me wish for a caesarian delivery;
it was already the Ides of March
when spring is in full view,
when oranges are done making their will,

and are lighting up the way to the blossoms of April;
yet behind the veil,
my orange wore a stern look,
as though to safeguard a modesty from stripping;
there was a new scent, pungently candid;

there was flesh voluptuous,
saintly voluptuous,
and there was the juice of plenty
so sweet
it compelled love on young and old.

The Two Sisters

Dimple-cheeked orange
submerged in the laughter of the leaves
reposed in the mist of the wave
and the embrace of the compassionate sun
taming sweet with your breath
the temper of heaven and earth
dimple cheek of high birth
yet always glad to glimmer ashore!

Your bigger sister, the grapefruit,
though soft-countenanced and smoother-skinned
she still wears the undiplomatic frown
over her abduction from her pagan abode,
and in her passionate blood
and her inviolate pouches
still reign and glitter
the odour and order of sky and sea.

Mothers of Jerusalem

Day is receding
autumnally
over the silent hills,
like the Mediterranean

as it ebbs down yonder,
away from its olive belt.
The vanguard of the twilight,
itself vanguard to pre-lapsarian dark

carries a mass of sound,
waving on the wane,
the air infiltrated to the core
by the breath of some evening cooking,

cauliflower being prepared the way
only the mothers of Jerusalem know
or by the spirit of select coal
yielded up affectionately

that they may iron
for the morrow of spouse and child:
it swells to the limit a heart
three-scores and ten thousand miles away.

The Wedding

They skipped to the time of the rope,
and the rope kept faith with their voice,
like crafting into one
the river's rhythm and the melody of the lake;

They sang as they skipped
of the still-forbidden to them,
of coffee dark and so beloved
whose wedding takes place
in young dainty cups
perfumed with the spirit of cardamom
in a home warm and fruitful,
they served but could not drink:
their dawn of knowing was at hand;

Their time and voice governed all about them
and far beyond:
the summer afternoon wind
toned down to listen,
and in amazement the sun
opened wide his eyes:
they panted
as they skipped and sang:

'Anal mahboobatussamra
wa-ujla fil fanajeeni
wa 'oudul Hindi lee 'itrun
wa thikree sha'a fisseeni.'

Time grew big
and space swelled wide:
all was heart there,
beating ever so loud,
skipping wild;

They danced on the threshold of day
and sang of sipping the scented drink,
of the wedding of bliss and grace.

In the Eclipse of the Moon

on a popular Arab song

We met beyond the wine of sunset
which causes the sky to blush
in the stillness between cool and warm;

there,
where heaven and earth wooed
and nearly mingled breath,

the moon hiding out of envy,
as she sensed the hair down her shoulders,
and the rose in her lips;

there, breathless
I asked of the road,
and the musk rose murmured it was still kind of long

along the road
which was all beginning,
all end;

there, I asked to quench my thirst,
and the jasmine gently urged
patience:

till the sugar had time to melt
in the virgin dew,
and the stillness ran out of breath.

Waiting for the Light in Nazareth

The light is not green yet,
and what if it were?
Ah, is that the breath from some bakery nearby?
The breath will for a long time delay the crossing,
make it unnecessary even;
it has the right of passage
laden with the best man has to offer;
it must go first
bearing the freshness of the field
and the days and works that went into its making,
red or green.

What does it matter
when she takes her stand at the corner,
the tray of fresh bread is still on her head,
her voice crisp with no summer in it yet,
her Galilean scent and manner
waved forth on the wings of a spring breeze,
her large eyes sparkling plenty yet untapped
beckoning those hungry for solace:

this is the truth
coeval with the primary fountain,
it informs every corner,
it cannot be sold,
it cannot be bought,
it can only be given
and only taken
when need so urges,
for love is the midwife of bread
and bread the nurse of love.

From Yafa

The lemon nods and dozes
in the sap-scented air
in the bright dreams of summer sun
soothing a child's silly fears
just a sweet distance from the palms
sweeter than the waves. The waves curl
like passion furling up in the falling cool;

Blush spreads, like a child's
innocent thought, it spreads borne high
by two stars robust and modest
to bless and partake of the ambient
crowned with dark curls. The curls wave
the purple perfume of the henna
and dreamily rouse to sparkling rave the seasoned sea.

Ear of Wheat

Ear of wheat arches
over the pitfalls of the dark
listening keenly to voices
gone by, to calls
drifting from afar,

ear of wheat bends
silent with weight
in front and back
silent with our weight of hours
with no before
with no after
and all around nothing
but the curt jitters and shivers in sun,

ear of wheat tosses in wind
sweating in calm
in narrow straits
teeming with yet far-reaching length and width,
golden ear laden
listening
up to the highest prominence
and, unaware,
through the petals of the night
the only friend of man
plowing through the evening,
of woman carrying the morning in her arms.

The Foundling

When *because* and *therefore* still looked
much like identical twins,
'You are not our son,'
say Father and Mother,
'We picked you up from the ditch.
Your father wears large shoes and a large hat!
No, you are not our son.'

And the not-son cries,
and the not-father and not-mother laugh,
and the more laughter,
the more tears,
and the more tears,
the more laughter;

and the boys laugh and say,
'He has no eyes.'
And when alone,
he touches his face,
and yes he has eyes,
and he wears no hat,
and his shoes are small,
much smaller than the shoes
his not-father wears;

but like his sisters, the boys
do not have to learn by heart
the words of the Holy Book,
and they were not found in any ditches,
and nobody beats them for not learning
by heart those crazy words,
as his not-father beats him,
and when he does not, he says,
'You are no good,
all you will do for a living
is to recite the Qur'an
at the cemetery
for a hardboiled egg and a piece of bread.'

It pleases the not-son.
He likes bread and hardboiled eggs:
it makes his not-mother quiet and sad;

and his sisters laugh and say
'He does not know yet how to eat.
He carries the food on the back of the spoon,'
and they laugh like the boys,

and the not-father says nothing,
and for a long, long time
he is quiet,
and the not-mother sobs
and sobs quietly
alone in the corner:

reason has not yet learned the art
of flowing from *because* to *therefore*:
'Is tears the cause of laughter,
or is laughter the cause of tears?'

Dafoura

Vanguard of the yield of the fig tree,
Dafoura awakes a bit ahead of her time
because of some restlessness in the blood

or illusion in the sky.
She swings with pubic ardour on the bough
over the fatal hour which falls short of dawn;

and, still innocent, she falls
as big as a small pomegranate
in the false light with a start on the cool harsh ground

missing that parting touch in the final rush of dark
which presses fullness on the fruit.
When dawn bursts forth at last a shade too late,

Dafoura feels close to a full-ripe fig,
Dafoura tastes almost as voluptuous
almost as sweet.

Uncle Haj Ali or the Ninety-Nine Names of God

Now clumsily,
now awkwardly,
the cat walks over the child's chest,
walks back and forth,
back and forth,
diagonally,
gingerly,
until she settles down
lengthwise over the child's chest;

And the rhythm and sound of her purring
soothe the child out of sleep
into a sweet half dream
of the cold outside,
of the dark outside,
and of the still untrodden faraway –

All before Uncle Haj Ali awakes
to say his prayers,
caress his rosary bead by bead,
seduce the air with the scent of bread
as he toasts it on a simple fire,
and walk the lonely road to work;
Uncle Haj Ali is the gentlest, kindest man
the town of Hebron has ever known:

When the child becomes a boy,
they teach him, and he likes what he learns
that apart from the cold and the dark and the call of the faraway,
the cat's purrings are the beads upon a thread
saying over and over
that all may heed
the ninety-nine holy names of God.

Her Temper

Whether it was the sun swooping down from the hills
or the wind sweeping from the Mediterranean
her temper remained the scent
of thyme waving on the slopes,
of the orange in modesty
waiting to be peeled into accents,
of cardamom ground fine
to refine the temper of the evening meal –
and on through the foliage of the silence
murmuring children of the new day.

My Aunt's Legacy

Her voice is the sum total
of seven modern decades:
The sun in the west toyed with
on the dark face by coarse wind,
her voice skirts the straight deaf course
and zigzags down to her niece
for a new set of decades.

Trial at Ramleh

The heat makes some room for the evening,
and a clamor filters through the distance
like cool water percolating through hard-yielding clay,
the sound and smell of the town, now as elemental
as the sound of pigeons and the smell of jasmine,
curl about every inch of the hour
and sink like dew in its thirsty flesh:

except for the quiet on the porch
where he sits down to some tobacco running low,
and where she putters about
resigned too far too soon:
An old man his humour strained thin
as though, with much on his head and more in his sides,
condemned to stand upright
upon an earthen pitcher of ill-tempered keel,
and his woman aging hard after him:
the awkward condensation of a once-perfect tale.

Peaches

The two peaches came from opposite orchards,
they waited to be picked up by some buyer or another;
it was late when the two men,
brothers in trade, arrived.
They examined the peaches and shook their heads:

'Who on earth would eat such peaches!'
exclaimed the one: 'One peach with so much sugar,
but with hardly any juice!
While the other with so much juice,
but with hardly any sugar!'

'You nailed it on the head,' agreed the other,
'just what I have been meaning to talk to you about:
I have a son,
and you have a son, right?
Your son is blind but smart,
my son is sighted but dumb!
Now is that fair, I ask you?
What would a dim-eyed person do with a brain?
Wouldn't God have done better
if he had given the brain of your son
to my son who sees but is a dim wit?
At least there would then be one good peach
don't you think so?'

Shocked, the other would-be buyer said,
'You must ask God that.'

The two peaches heard all that, and nodded as if to say,
'The Lord giveth, and the Lord taketh away.'
'I wouldn't for the world,
sweet sister, covet your sugar!'
'Nor would I for the whole world,
my good sister, covet your juice!'

Progress of the Sun

Ordered the despot of the East,
when he was told that the convict was too tall
for the tree on which he was to hang,
ordered he that a shorter man be found,
so that he might hang in his place:

and men were speechless with fear,
and the sun came out all disheveled that morning;

said the wise judge of the West,
when he learned that the convict was too young
for either the injection or the chair,
'Why,' said he, 'keep him in custody
until he is old enough.'

And men and women bubbled with applause,
and the sun that evening washed in dirty water.

Boasting

My nephew claims that he shook hands with the president,
the born-again president
who was lit up when my nephew sang for him!
Imagine!
He shook hands with the president!

Now my uncle swears that he kissed the hand,
it was hairy,
which may have later shaken the hand
of no other figure
than that madman, bad for all time!

My aunt is rich but bald,
she always boasts of the rich hair
of her otherwise poor maternal cousin.
And I who have spent my life courting poverty,
I am very proud of my aunt's wealth!

Kind of reminds you, doesn't it,
of our neighbour who is proud
to ecstasy on hearing that our Milky Way,
yes, our own Milky Way, is in the process
of swallowing up its neighbour, the Andromeda.

Mother And Child

'Crash!' goes the whip,
and the night jumps out of her sleep,
crash in the mighty father's hands,
and we scare in our beds
outside the pale of the whip
in the big night
and Ahmad calls in breaking voice:
'Mother!'
'Mother!' before swish –
'Mother!' after crash...

In the night where the moon is full and the stars bright
cringe he does
as 'crash' screams the lash
like the winds that lose all temper
and vow to flush out the secret of the heart,
and Ahmad writhes and calls,
and the warm night shivers with us in the silence,
she contracts with fright
like the flesh under lash
before it swells in pain,

and faraway still under moon and stars,
the woman keeps faith
the woman keeps watch,
as she crouches on the white sand
and listens by the waves,
she hears children's voices breaking out
on the wings of the salty winds,
now lisping now sibilant,
now whispering now harsh –
'Mother!'

Mother on a shore forlorn
where in their play rough or gentle
the waves flash no less matter
than her child does in his:
in the swish and the whisper,
in the harsh crash,
and the whims of the winds in sway,
while the mother prays in vain
to the father of wave and child
'Mother'...

For We Know Not What We Do

To breathe the image of a heifer
and then move back a step or two
in order to look at the creation,

only to start
realizing it says more than you said,
does differently from how you do,

points with the head in directions
you apprehend a little more
than does the spark its offspring of fires and fires;

it further carries in the eyes
shapings of that faraway
which float only into the ken of the Olympian Bull

whom the child once surprised dozing,
leapt thoughtlessly on his back,
took him by the golden horns –

and the shock of ignition!
It bellowed the earth out of breath,
it dazzled the sky's eyes.

Under the Sycamore Tree

How stubbornly it surfaces
through the veil and cover of fifty years
still as soft as a gossamer,
how faithfully it surfaces

each time I hold a hammer or mallet
driving my hand to the edge of shaking or shuddering!
Yes, even before reaching awakening,
sleep swiftly curdles into death;

there in the shadow of the tall sycamore tree
the hammer's vanguards,
two blinded children of a blind progenitor,
they sink in the skull

sink fast and deep
they claw their way with startling ease
as if through layers of curds
she has fallen in love

blind love they say
fallen out of her faith
out of custom
out of character,

her lover belongs to the enemy camp:
in dark rage her brother says *no*
at least out of character
out of stubborn custom;

blind fury in her hand
fells him out of sleep,
and he falls straight into a deeper sleep,
the lover is fled it is said

fearing a similar fate:
and for once the blind father sees
as he is being led into the shade
of the spreading sycamore tree –

And for fifty years,
stubbornly arrested between
the rage of a hammer's sharp drive,
and the wrath of its blunt weight.

The Orphan

for my parents

...and then the newly widowed woman
said in a voice somber and shaky,
'I kissed his hand,
as he was still lying in bed,
his eyes closed
like the eyes of a child sound asleep:

I said to him (I am sure he heard me),
"you were always kind to me,
may your soul rest in peace;
for fifty years you brought me happiness:
may every wife be made
as happy as you made me;

you loved me,
you provided for me
so that our home never knew need,
you sheltered me from the cold of winter
and from the heat of summer:
may the bliss of paradise be your reward;

and when misfortune struck
and robbed our first born of light,
and people whispered or looked strange
as if we were come from a different world,
you stood by me unquestioning, unwavering
maintaining to the end it was all the will of God.

And if I ever did you wrong,
I bear all the blame,
even though I intended no wrong:
forgive me, your humble and ever-loving wife,
may heaven be your final abode,
and may we still meet there again."

It was Friday, and he who had bathed him asked,
"How many times was he a pilgrim?"
"He never went on pilgrimage," I said,
"How could that be!
Never went on pilgrimage
when his bathwater was so musk-scented?"

'Son, it is always the will of God,
An orphan since five, motherless and fatherless
Did he not find you orphan and give you shelter?
Did he not find you erring and show you the right path?
Did he not find you needy and give you plenty?'"
The rest was bathed in tears.

II

The Spider

After a tradition in the life of the Prophet Muhammad

When night seemed to gain the upper hand,
faith guided them into the cave
which brimmed with life that had sought
sanctuary there from the heat
of the barren sun and from the desert
ever so blood-thirsty.
The cave glittered with the shine of the reptilian dance
while outside, the dark was fattening
on the hunger of widow and orphan.

In the cave weary Abu Bakr
fell down breathless,
he stretched out his legs as far as they could reach,
and the Teacher laid his head upon his thigh
and fell into a deep sleep
as deep as his cousin's in His deserted bed.
It was dark outside,
you could not see your hand,
but you could hear the clink-clink
of the chains on foot and hand.

Wary Abu Bakr, the sweat
playing on his brow and beard,
gazed about him, and struggled hard
to keep his heart from sinking: His faith
was gold with but a shallow scratch,
and that caused the adder's nip at the bare heel.
The desert outside was a vast grave,
grinning as it swallowed alive the infant girl.

Abu Bakr's tears joining his sweat
pebbled down big upon his companion's cheek.
The Teacher awoke
and with his spittle held the venom at bay:
his faith did not waver
not by a sliver of a sunbeam,
faith the ladder when perfect
to full knowing
to full understanding.

For three nights the two men listened
to the arguments of their pursuers
swarming about the cave's mouth
like a horde of sterile sand
about to assault your teeth:
'They must be in.'
'They cannot be.'
'Where else can they be?'
'Just look at the inviolate web at the gate.'
For three dark days they argued
in a desert of soul and mind
until the stars, sun and all
hid their faces and shut tight their ears.
Teacher and Disciple listened among forked tongues
which played about them in a swirl of slime
'Will they come in, Teacher?'
'The weave is a thousand shields strong.'
'And these dreadful creatures?'
'They dance with joy over what is to come.'
'Are we two match to the hordes outside?'
'There is a third with us.'

On the fourth day the virgin cave was due:
like the primal flash of light
at that primary moment
at the start of time
the two men burst through the web
which the patient spider had woven
at the gate out of her very being:

there the light bursting,
a slice of heaven
to tame fast the dark
to dispel the night,
there the ever-expanding
ever-teeming slice of moon.

By the Sacred Cave

Based on a tradition possibly initiated by Abu Huraira who was a follower of the Prophet Muhammad.

The vast silence reigned there,
and led her tiny feet toward the place,
right near the mouth of the solitary cave,
among the listening rocks,
beneath the outskirts of the departing sun;

he was utterly silent,
as if in sleep,
but she heard him,
she heard all
as she softly approached to receive the blessing;

the cloak which clothed him spread large,
and on the cloak she lay and fell to praying:
she lay there and prayed without taking off
her coat of fur softer than a child's dream.
Though neither was aware,
his meditations and her prayers joined,
as they soared upward
toward the coveted gate,

the silence there embraced all,
the child-like rattles in her chest and up her throat
felt the awe which the silence swayed,
and the sound went down
down until nothing was heard,
and she fell
into a meditation-like sleep;

this brought him back to where she lay
right by his side in prayer or a dream,
he too looked and saw all:
the cloak now was as much his as hers,
and gratitude swelled his heart up to the throat;

and though neither knew it,
out of each
a blessing flowed for the other,
and rather than disturb the grace upon her face,
he cut from the cloak
the part on which she lay,
and softly, very softly
he left, scarcely hearing his footsteps;

and ever since,
whenever her fellow cats purred
'Where did you get this unearthly carpet?'
She purred back, 'From that place
near the sacred cave
where divinity and 'felinity'
together always pray.'

Bilal

'Enough of the Muslims and their veils...' they murmur,
'and does not this call to prayer
give us the creeps as it echoes

and further echoes through the four corners of the earth?
Enough of the Blacks,' they grumble,
'Does not the sight give us the dark shivers

as they rise and thicken around us?
But the horror, the real horror is when
Black and Muslim together fall prostrate,

fall as one on soft and hard
their prayer rising, spreading
like a global flower flourishing

to overwhelm and abolish
the unnatural weeds which breed
the unnatural haves and have-nots.'

'We are awed by the lightning
in your gentle eyes, Bilal,
you first Black of the Muslims,

lighting which pierces deep beyond the eye
its Allahu Akabar swelling the throat of the sky
dissipating the murk and grime around us

it leaves us naked in the light
how we fear the thunder
in the sweetest of voices, Bilal!

Voice composed of strength and sweetness
compressed into one
your all-penetrating voice, Bilal!

You, father of the lofty minaret
owner of the voice which reigns from sunrise to sunset
voice as luxuriant as your hair

you, first Muslim of the Blacks,
thunder which tames the rage of the heart,
its Allahu Akabar filling the chest of heaven!

Steadfast call which quells the mutiny in the blood
and reins in the malignant cells
that rage under veil of white

it knits into one
blonde and brunette
yellow and brown

it shatters the dark and myopic manacles
it thaws the ice which wraps itself around the mind,
you vocal beamer to earth and sky

of the word of God
of the mercy of God
of the love of God

faith – all light – colourblind, and genderless
it brings forth one great soul –
one human race!'

Observations

Light eternal,
fire eternal,
flower eternal
eternally being,
eternally increasing
the will to know and understand,
the ardour to generate and propagate,
and true love without bounds:

in a tide of light
the first bore him,
no one else could,
and delivered to the world a promise;

in times lean and dry
the second nursed the shepherd-to-be,
no one else would,
and fecund went the land;

the third, ardent and steadfast,
ensured that the new-born faith
would increase against the winds of darkness
and she bore the fourth to the world,

who in turn ensured that his blood,
he was human to the core,
would run for all time
strong in the human stream:

Ah, the seeds planted in the soil of promise
and nursed in infinite dream!
Ah, the blossoms sheltered and fed in hope,
and the burst in flower for all!

IV
If our Prophet did not know all,
and who but the Creator knows all,
still he knew so much,
he did not mind the bestowal
of illiteracy upon him,
and that so excited the moon
she shown full bright at mid-day;

we who uphold the faith today,
and that's what the Prophet did not know,
know so little that we believe
it is a heavenly virtue to be illiterate
taking our unknowing to be the Prophet's,
and that so embarrasses the sun
he pales and takes up the veil.

This Noon

'And say, Lord, have mercy on both of them [my parents]
even as they raised me when I was little'
al Qur'an Sura 17.

A beginning disowned
and an end discarded
only beget a dismal middle

this noon is the rising of the day
he despoils the infant of his grandeur
and dumps him at the babysitter's

this noon is the sunset whom
he strips of his grave dignity
and has him half-buried in a nursing home:

this noon's character
must be highly questionable
for all the majesty he strains to beam;

the prime is not the prime
unless it is as much the prime
as it is the spring and fall,

the race is the race only
when it keeps its childhood in full
when it keeps its old age intact;

and you, look how you still tower from the high hour
as you munch on your buds and fruition
as you feed and feast on yourself!

The Palm Tree

'Do not grieve, your Lord has set a rivulet beneath you,
shake toward you the trunk of the palm tree:
Ripe dates will fall upon you'
al Qur'an Sura 19, Mariam

Sound is her sleep like his
sounder than the sea and deeper
in the shadow of the palms
beautiful and barren
American palms they call them over there,
and they banish out of sight the palms
which bare hunger-taming fruit,
the fruit drops through the dawn
soft and cool, moist and sweet
it nourished long ago
in their harsh exile
a mother and her tide-bearing child –

Fecund is the tide and inexhaustible
it governs into one
the rhythms of wave and cloud
it guides the stone distracted out of context
back to the firm rock of being
it returns from its long exile of stain and taint
the drop of water to the spring incorruptible
it gives back to the moment its magnitude of time:
Then bring back home the banished palm
shake the trunk of the palm
it will drop tranquility
it will rain peace.

Out of Bondage

He lay among the sheep all night,
yes and he did not know any better,
He breathed in the odour of their dirt
where water is scarce,
but I take a shower every day;

He bowed too low for the screen
in order to revel
in the chastity of the unwashed
where the sky is too dry for tears,
and I take two showers a day;

He stood, a thief between two thieves,
his smell overwhelmed the smell of death,
but his companions were not subdued,
rather they held their noses bent on sleeping in,
and I take three showers a day;

He asked for water when his throat went dry
and his blood was running out,
and when heaven would give none,
they offered him the bitter drink,
and thus unfettered and unwashed I took the open road.

Easter Poem

Is it really here
finally here?
She asked part mournful part in hope:
the red-breasted robin has stationed himself
here, right here
in the bosom of the olive tree,

and he calls with the passion
of the sun in his descent and rising
he calls full-throated to the honeysuckle,
that divine commoner,
to rise from her sleep and beam
to the world her full-scented dream
of the weed learning from the rose
and the mosquito from the butterfly.

To a Poisoned Girl

Pardon me!
but what you wear today
is only the memory of a manger
cleansed long ago of its baby
and of all the baby's siblings who dwelt there!

What you have on at best
parodies the dung of the lowly
minus the earthiness
which a baby from purest heaven
once came down to do homage to!

What you wear stirs up
only a grossly edited version
of what long ago
a virgin witnessed and embodied
unpurified and unrefined!

What you have on today is of a saintly chemistry
processed well beyond the human:
it lacks the dirt, the innocent dirt
so necessary for tomorrow's grace,
hence you are poisoned!

The Magic Fruit

She sat at His gleaming feet
within a forenoon hour of Palestine,
she listened in ecstasy,
her eyes sparkling as she studied His words
which had a straight and easy way to the centre of the soul,
a fragrant flower adoring the rising sun,
her spirit whetting its wings for unshackled flights
into worlds of beauty and purity
of sweetest thought and sweetest sound and sweetest sight,
worlds beyond the grasp of our understanding,
beyond the hills and the olive trees...

Beyond the kitchen grouching and fretting
with her sister's sweat and greasy hair,
her sleeves rolled up in her labour
now loud of breathing
now out of breath
amidst a multitude of odours
of competing detergents,
labour which achieves cleanliness
and feeds a hungry household,
self-sacrifice in the interest
of our daily living:

Between the busy kitchen and the tranquil living room,
between sweetness and usefulness
sat an old woman and beside her
a basket of bright oranges
on a low table made of stone,
their breath whispering about
the perfume of maturity
in a golden sunset of Palestine.
The old woman babbled like a child
about how when still a child
she fell asleep on the road issuing
from the City of God and dreamt
she was in heaven because it smelt like heaven
on the road from Jerusalem to Yafa,
Yafa, city of sweet oranges by the sparkling waves,
Yafa, bride of the everlasting sea;

And the month was April
when the old woman had her dream,
month of orange blossoms,
of the birth of the golden orange which spends
half the year out-perfuming the rose,
and the other half out-doing the olive
in increase, in utility:

Fruit of the sacred flesh!
It instructs the daughter of beauty to wonder:
What use is the noble rose
without the apple and the peach!
What use the grace
of a pair of heavenly luminaries
without woman awkwardly great with life!
It teaches the daughter of industry to ask at last:
Why not the breath of cello or violin
to temper the hoarse pantings
of a carpenter's tireless saw?
May not the cup of gold blush
with wine and serve water too?

It charms even the vision of the Teacher
of all teachers from Palestine
into seeing wedded each to each
God swinging on a tree and the grain-grower
caught in the swayings of the seasons,
in the hallowed fragrance of the orange
which knits the members of the year
into a wholesome whole,
life at its perfection!
Magic fruit
begotten of the human and the divine,
you who weave into one
the bee and the butterfly!

The Pity of it

for Abu al-ʿAla

When the blind poet entered the second prison
and settled behind the second wall,
the veil fell off his face,
a tooth abscessed or grown old,
the torment began in earnest:
established truth shook like a moth-eaten faith.
The double prisoner saw all,
and all but wept,
and he wished us out of faith that we might see.

Year after year the Hebrews have claimed
their father Abraham
came close to slitting the throat of Isaac
as if he were a sheep –
keen was the knife like a peak deserted in hunger
so that for all his dignity
the sun babbled about a bloody feast
and Isaac son of Abraham was not unwilling,
all because of blind faith, and faith is said to be blind.

Year after year the Muslims have maintained
their ancestor Ibraheem was on the point
of cutting the throat of Isma'eel his son
as though he were a young, tender-fleshed camel –
keen was the blade like a desert thirst
so that the cold moon
nearly dropped her solemn vows
and Isma'eel in blind trust was not unwilling,
all because of man's love for God.

Guilty or not
poor Abraham and his prime sons!
How their offspring, truthful or not,
put their necks on the line!
God, they barely made it!
Women would then have ceased to bear
and men would have plowed in vain
and in discord everywhere –
what else in such distraction of sun and moon?

Year after year the Christians,
resolved not to be outdared,
have asserted the father of mankind
let Jesus be nailed and speared by angry men
as he hung on an olive tree
and the whole creation wept
and Christ saw all, and cried for all his faith
'Father, why hast thou forsaken me?'
this time all because of God's love for man!

Eve

Laughter and tears, the wise tell us,
spring from the same fountain:
is not a child still a child
whether, as he plays, he goes on his feet or on his head?

So, engulfed or immersed
in their oral reverie,
how else could it be,
under an overcast sky,

'My father is a lost soul,'
says Abraham to his companion,
'Lost in an unholy fire!
But never will I mourn him!'

'My son is a lost soul,'
says Noah to his companion,
'Lost to waves which wash no soul!
But never will I mourn him!'

Thus runs their conversation
as they sit, all unknown to them,
between 'the devil and the deep blue sea,'
when all at once the sun comes out.

III

For Now

As Jerusalem edged toward the brink

For now the foliage and the rough-playing wind
muffle their high voices
among the violets –

an assembly in euphoria
the riot in their blood
and the spirit in their feet;

they spring
higher than the aspiring wheat
they shout in its yet-unformed ears

phrases brief and drawn-out
property to all
owned by none;

they pant
like the breath of lilac
in a reflective sun

after their rising shadows
after birds of sparse humour
after sky not out of dream's reach;

to be quickened by the wings of *Immisliman*
Grasshopper and Butterfly
and agile Prophet's Mare

yet as happy as they may be
the afternoon already leans on an incline
a bit irritable in the sides,

as merry as they may make the air
the hills about them seem to know too much
and keep still –

for now the grass is barely above its birth
its ardour though held in check
far outweighs its age,

for now the foliage and the wind at play
absorb their voices as luxuriant wool
absorbs the tinklings of a throng of bells.

Remembrance of an Old Spring

Rickety is the sun,
the young year's bones damaged from within,
neither the bright fruit of the grove
nor the air perfumed with its breath
can dispel the apprehension:

behind, the sore feet and buttocks of the mountains,
like a child's who hasn't done his lessons,
are still bare and swollen from the whippings of winter,
and the peaks aren't done smarting
from the screeching and scratching of the winds:

before, the shallow sky, like a boy
who hasn't yet learned how to interpret scars,
hangs over the liquid expanse
where so much is iffy, you would think
the very how and what of being were in doubt.

In Exile

Though not perfect, many considered the procedure,
as we call it these days,
a great success, some even
call it a miracle;
after all, aren't we now in the land
that used to be fertile with miracles?
She herself didn't know what to make of it;

as for her son,
he learned nothing of her tongue,
if he did when he was young,
he forgot it all;
contrary to instinct or tradition,
he thought of seeking no roots;

his mother was young when she came to the strange land
to live among aliens,
the fascists killed her husband
and drove her out of her faraway land;
it took quite a while before she could adjust
to the new tongue planted in her mouth,
'tongue transplant' they told her;
it was a strange tongue
which continued to be heavy to the end of her life:

she sold peanuts in the heart of the City,
close to the Holy Sepulchre,
'Peanuts to your delight,' she chanted as she roasted,
in an accent so foreign, and so delightful,
'Peanuts fresh from Ethiopia,
land of the steadfast sun
and of the starful skies,'
she roasted and chanted
until all around her and far beyond
grew light with the breath of the perfect roast;

and the men and women relished her peanuts,
and were amused by her foreignness,
but bothered themselves with no roots;
the children, as if enchanted,
clustered about her,
breathed in the roasted air,
ate peanuts to their delight,
and would, if they could,
make their tongues perform like hers;

she sold
until she grew tired,
often wondering at how the new sun and stars
looked different like her new tongue in her mouth,
and now there is a telephone in the house,
the miraculous telephone,
but to her disappointment
nobody calls for her,
not even her son calls;
her people who live far away...
what 'people!' she starts checking herself,
she has no people...
'Ah, probably they don't have telephones,
else surely they would call,'
and they would wonder at her new tongue
were they to hear her
just as the people over here wonder;
'My new tongue!
I can't reach into the past with it!
How it points to things I don't get!
Strange things!'

She grows old as does the air
which used to bear and spread the fragrance of the roast,
all that is left to her,
fragments of simple tunes
which she hums to herself now and then,
and she is surprised when she cannot tell

whether one tune or the other
is foreign or her people's;
she has but one wish left,
the wish to teach her son to say three things
in her old tongue
just in case one of the three circumstances
prevents her from answering the phone herself,
provided he is there
on one of his rare visits,
she would teach her son to say
in her old and discarded tongue,
'Mother is in the shower,
Mother is out,
Mother is dead.'

Coal to Cardiff

The stranger's arrival coincided
with that of an abnormal wind
which vexed the scent of the air
as would a cloud of dust an unsuspecting eye,
or a foreign insect the petals of a flower;

none of us boys knew where the stranger came from,
from the City of Light,
from the City of Dreams,
or just from the city of enterprise:

he came, and planted himself among us,
only to spread our music among us, he said,
to teach us how to enjoy it and even make it!
His name was Azouri,
a Jew everybody said –
that was before the desert was to bloom,
before the miracle at Fecund Damona.

'Bringing music to us!'
Jameel of Gaza exclaimed,
'Don't we have Sami Al-Shawwa
and his great violin which the whole country knows and
loves?'
Soon there was perfect accord
that 'the English and the Jews' were bringing us
many things we already had or did not want:

Oranges to Yafa,
city of bright oranges,
bride of the white waves!
Olives to the city
which hosts the Mount of Olive!
But 'you can't bring coal to Cardiff!'

Grapes to Hebron whose vines
had flourished long ago and used to satisfy
the thirst and hunger of Abraham!
Dates to the palm tree
whose fruit nourished the Mother of God!
But 'you can't bring coal to Cardiff!'

Bread of seductive colours
to Nazareth and its Galilee
of the gold-waving wheat!
Even soap to Nablus
city of the miraculous soap!
But 'you can't bring to coal to Cardiff!'

Until the wisest boy among us
took us all by surprise with his announcement
that the English, 'masters of mankind,'
were going to bring a better brand of faith to Palestine;
they would, if they could
bring us another Jesus!
They would verily bring their sun
to enlighten 'the gorgeous East!'
But, of course 'you can't bring coal to Cardiff!'

While Azouri was writing music for us,
Arabic music!
He must have come from some city of sound!
It was music, we were taught,
which was 'refined, scientifically made!'
Yet, in truth, hearing it, would either throw us into deep sleep,
or repel us like an ominous odour
that had invaded the air we breathed!
It was a music like – when another boy interrupted
'like the rose which stood erect and tall
scentless, with its heart wrenched out,
extracted like a tooth!'

To the Lemon

So keen, you sting wild the sea, your neighbour,
and shake his white beard big with little pride:
so sharp you set on edge
the teeth and buds of a whole generation:
so seductive your breath borne on the wind,
it almost alters heaven's chemistry.

Yet, as though to prove you remain
central among the community of beings,
if the north had its way as it sometimes does,
you stand as much a chance as a baby orphan might.
And we might have guessed as much
had we but had the sense to heed your blossoms.

The Betrayal of Joseph

'Now it is his turn,
the blind boy's turn,'
in a whisper just below the talk of the waves,
and soon after the brief bloody scuffle at day's end.
The sun is abashed,
as the sky bears a face not so pleasant.
'His father is already far away
with neither eyes to see nor ears to hear –'
The sun drowned a distance ago in the west,
in the darkening thirst of the waves,
and the mournful seal which spreads
like a malignant stain.

The surf pounds and swells
as it pants after the beach,
a heart quite disturbed,
unlike the boy's heart
lying on the sand frightened white;
the surf surges upwards
gaining upon the beach
sheet beyond sheet,
layers upon layers of sand
rising up to the neck,
and the heart pounding to beat off the weight,
the sand leaves free the sightless eyes
that they may interpret the approaching sound,
grunts like waves of angry crows
pecking at the Judassed dusk.

Just a joke, not a prank,
played by a bunch of boys:
at such an hour
it is too early to tell
one colour from another.

The breath of a keen spirit
thirsts upward and forward
waving toward the boy
waiting under his weight of white.
It leaves him with one ear that still hears
the boyish voices long fled east
giggling into the silence
over the dwindling beach;
with the other ear to hold out
against the foam-ridden billows and the tide-armoured night.

Dead End

God! The trees which blossom and bloom and bear no fruit!
Bellows busy fanning cold fires!
Billows stirring up dead seas!

How they spread all over town and country!
How they shoot up ever higher and higher
with smiles, and zeal, and skyward dreams!

How majestic they swell and sway in midsummer
clean, pure, and without odour!
Like someone always busy with great beginnings,
dizzy over dead ends!

How they endure at labour,
like the special children of golden asses and divine steeds!

God! The shades they pledge to provide!
The ardour with which they make their pledges!
How sweetly they lure the birds only to break their hearts
with contraceptives as safe as science can conceive!

In May

It was in May,
and who does not remember May
when promises are on the brink of bloom?
Yes, May the month whose mirth and merriment
almost touch the outskirts of holiness?

It was then that a group of blind boys
took it into their heads
to march from the City of Father Abraham,
their city to the village
which promised them an afternoon of rest
from sweat and thirst and hunger.

They marched to the new time
of what they had just learned in class
'And when she was good,
she was very, very good,
and when she was bad,
she was horrid!'
'That's you,' said little Hamdi,
'Aren't you blind?
Everybody knows
when a blind boy is good,
he is, for some reason, the best,
and when he is bad,
why, he is, for yet another reason, the worst!'

They marched on,
as the sun was waxing impatient,
they were close to their promised reward,
when suddenly they ran
into a rustic who innocently asked,
'And where is this army of blind men heading?'

'And a good army it is!'
fired back a voice from among the troops
the army of blind boys marched on,
seeing neither light nor dark,
their blindness transcending both.

Does it really matter then
whether it is 'ignorant armies clashing by night'
or just 'a blind man bettering blind men?'

And on the brink we rested,
and there we ate lamb chops,
and there we drank buttermilk,
it was so good after the May heat,
before the great leap and the long, long march.

Just Around the Corner

I
The vine will still be half-savage
with none of the art of climbing to her credit,
abandoned like an unwanted child
she will crawl between June and July
with teats sour and shrill
bitching at a hive of cold dark,
long overdue for change;

the road will be half-buried
under the pulse-dead stone,
it will be lonely
in the animated silence
exceptionally lonely
save for a fly on the wing
singing over the memory of urine
fast fading out of character
through age and the beating of the sun –

and a boy as if out of his mind there
marking keen and impatient blood,
just around the corner.

II
We walked in broad daylight,
we could not see,
as happy as children,
the path was deserted
the path was narrow

a strip so narrow
there was scarcely room for your foot,
we did not know,
nothing strange,
we moved with the certainty of the all-seeing,

time too was a narrow strip
growing ever narrower
we thought it was infinity
dumped in a well dry and abandoned
nothing funny
nothing eerie:
it was all just around the corner.

III

The sudden fall and explosion
of the dark on a cluster of boys
in bright circle,
so closely knit
you would think they were one,
all at once
the circle are the shrapnel of the dark,

they dart
upon diverse dark paths,
one only is left behind
alone on a slither of circle
forsaken, betrayed,
at first as if becalmed in the breathless silence,

then the frightening sound
of the frightened feet
frightened by a teeming void
eager to gain and turn the corner.

IV

Song of Songs

Let me watch how you orphan the planet
with your ingenious scourges
and I will make some sketches,

let me go with you
when you go hunting your bird or beast
so that I may make a drawing,

let me watch you do your raping
and please let me come as close as is decently possible
in order to make an indelible etching,

and pray let me in on the process of bone-splitting
from hidden springs to mouth gaping
and let me hear the dialogue between the two actors
until the whole matter is forced out and settled
and I will do a full painting
it will immortalize all –

and now that I am so seasoned, so civilized
I will take part in that act which flays alive a childhood
and brings to some rotten end the autumn of an old age
ah, that will do it!
It will enable me to write my poem,
my song of songs.

After the Long March

for Mutih

Hand in hand they stand at the corner
his crisp and dewy
hers wrinkled like a ringed bark
they stand at the last crossing after the long march
they see the yet unseen and hear the unheard
at the corner it is cold
but exceptionally quiet and clear

abruptly his hand shakes loose from hers
the lights across beckon
the sounds of rejoicing urge
he skips like the *shunnar* of the land
rolling up time and distance
in order to gain the other side
achieve another age

she follows slowly, determined
the hallowed oak on her back and the primeval evergreen
he looks back for her for the last time
her eyes after him
before him
beyond him
on the rainbow decorating him white, black, red, green

suddenly the flash the din and the dimness
through the eye at the birth of dawn
instantly the fall in the dizzy drains of darkness
at the very threshold of the new state,
root and bough torn apart
on the verge of bloom
torn with the spite of an age losing out
it was said the mother of that dawn
could no longer make sense since his fall

fall of leaves on their own turf
kneaded in blood and earth
they enshrine the sacrifices of the generations
they raise and make fecund the sunrise.

At Sitti's

The flies were countless that summer day,
and, ignoring the quality of mercy,
we killed them mercilessly;
even the blind boy had no pity then;
we killed them,
and they lay on the worn-out mat,
dark brown pearls,
as we later learned how to think of it;
we killed them
where we were learning
how to read and revere the word of God.

Suddenly the old teacher
put an end to the massacre,
when her voice swelled big the room
'Who wants to swallow the word of God today?'
and all went rolling on the tired mat
eager to swallow the word of God,
we rolled and rolled toward her
among her many chickens
and over their droppings wet and dry;

And by design or accident
it was the blind boy's turn to win
a tiny bit or shred of paper
bearing the name of God
which God only knows where she got it,
he swallowed
and hope surged up,
'Sitti, will God now make me able to read?'
'Hush,' as the necklace on her neck tinkled,
'God will yet do something good for you';

and He did that afternoon
when the planes of the English came flying over us,
but dropped no bombs,
because the blind boy had swallowed the name of God;
Sitti was scared,
and when the plane flew away,
her fear turned into rage:
Her deprecations fell out of her mouth
like rocks without control:
'May God break the nation of the English,
may God destroy them all,
may God strike them blind,
may God's blessings never come their way!'
But we were sorry no bombs came down.

'The chickens did not lay today,'
she said in her loud voice to her old husband,
as we were on our way out.

At the Village

During the Palestine uprising against the British

Winter's free winds and its naked limbs
touch and make merciless moan,
yet they give the lull to every mother's sleep;

In spring the neighbour's dog howls,
gloom spreads intimate in the night,
and haze lies still, suspended between earth and sky;

The dog howls all night long again,
it rocks the sleep of bird and beast;
in time of spring a poor dog knows more than he should:

The engines growl low as they glide into the third night,
the boom and rattle silence the prattling throat,
they sail away roaring a song of shattered hearts;

Through apple blossoms, the mercy machine wails in;
before the dew dies, it wails away
to bring them back neither to winter nor to spring.

Awad

A free translation

Let night tarry a little
until the prisoner tells his grief,
for hanging he shall swing in the breezes
on the flutter of dawn's wings.

Let not night come to an end
before I recount my sorrows,
night, the forgetful witness to my dark hours,
to the shattering of the cup of communion.

I cry not for fear of dying,
but for fear for my country,
and for a bunch of chicks in a house forlorn and hungry.
Ah, who will feed them when they have already
hanged my two young brothers?

My wife! Oh how I dread the days which await her!
Woe to me and to her little ones!
If only I had left her the bracelets she wore on her arm,
when in obedience to the call of struggle I sold them to buy arms!

Disgrace to the monarchs on whom we counted!
Their crowns are not fit to sole our boots:
alone must we now defend our country,
alone must we dress her wounds.

The Beam

On the hanging by the British of Sheikh Farhan al-Saʿdi

Did they embrace in the breath
of the bedewed jasmine and virgin coffee,
the dim-eyed woman and the four-score man
before he gasped his last, thirsty in his holy fast,
his name already flickering in the memory,
hers hushed from the start?

Did they whisper their vows once more
as they had done long ago,
before wrong came of age
and the sea overflowed with murk and blood
and the land choked with smoke of unholy flames,
vows made in the intimacy
of young henna and fresh thyme?

Did they, now that he had crossed
the zone of fear and wrath and sorrow
and was all but ready to walk
head high, smiling, impatient to meet his maker,
to hang upon a beam made all the more grim
by wrath-infected aliens
who make it their holy business
to hound the earth with their infection
leaving behind them numberless trails of blood and tears?
Did the supplications of church bells
and of the calls from the minaret
fail to move those powers
reigning supreme over there?
Were the pleadings of mother and tender child
powerless to awaken mercy from her slumber?
Did the tongue, after he had instructed his eldest
son to remember mother, brothers and sisters,
did the tongue then come out white

in the musty room shaded from the budding beams,
from the hills bowed low,
from the brooks drying up,
from the fire winding down, winding down?

Did he inspect for the last time
with the apprehension of final vision
the long processes of the years,
years passed and years yet to come
slouching with their deliveries
of self-perpetuating cruelty?

Did he swing heavy upon the beam,
denied the basil-scented
lilac-scented air,
denied the sight and voice
of light-hearted children
beaming from their swings?

Manning the Door:
an Elegy for Ibrahim Abu-Lughod

I

Nightmare by the foam surging
now white now black
and shapes at the door pushing in
and I pushing back
shapes born not on this earth
they dance to the time which drives sleepless
the waves, my childhood friends
shapes generated by no man
born of no woman
come to outdo the wrath of wind and fire

they push in
I push back
in the seesaw of ebb and tide
and the waves my childhood friends they make sinister snorts
I utter a loud cry
above the cry of wind and surf
none seems to heed or hear
and I start chest-gripped out of sleep

you need sleep says the doctor
you need peace
peace of childhood waves
in the face of the shapes that are bred
on the froth of the sea
come ashore to consume the very earth
foaming froth ceaselessly pushing
to break in and force the rivers
to devour our support

and the sea growls and gurgles
to the shapes hissing ashore
I start breathless out of sleep
I cry for help at the sight
at the door by the shore
and all around me listening...deaf
and all around me watching...blind

then I curse the sea my boyhood brother
for casting ashore such monstrous shapes
peace my friend shrills the doctor,
'Rest, rest is what you need,' he gutters at the door
they hiss ashore foaming lies
truth being all alien to them
they boast they are children of God
they push in, I push back by the faithless waves.

II

Now your labour is over brother
the nightmare is over
and you are back home
laid to rest by the spring
in the place of your childhood dreams
it is a reality that your heart has ceased to beat
a reality hard to come to terms with
it is the loss of a major limb

but it is the truth that your blood
continues to flow strong and healthy
unbowed you have returned to the fountain
which inspired you before your exile
and which for more than five decades
gave you steadfastness for a drink
and unstinting you gave to your disciples
for decades you wandered over the face of the earth
restless and tireless like the waves
bearing the terror and the weight of our nightmare
constantly manning the door
the door ceaselessly rocking to and fro

you never wavered or lost direction
never lost sight of the ultimate destination
wherever you went
and under whatever circumstance
you taught Yafa stubbornly
you preached Jerusalem stubbornly
to the grave dismay
of the *Viracochas* and their relations
and for all the great minds you were at home with
you were because of your humility
as much the learner from the unlettered and the poor

you were a realist to the hilt
when the waves rose out of bound
you let them bear you on their crest
but you were steadfast to the last syllable
wherever you went
you ate *hummus* and *falafel*
olive oil and thyme
and you drank Arabic coffee
and always smelt like a fresh orange from Yafa
where things began...

you were the tough gristle
which for forty years America could not chew
until fearing you would choke her
she cast you out
not like the froth of the sea
but as the sea's cleanser of its froth
and for all your toughness brother
your heart like a child's would melt with pity
at the sight of a bird in distress
or a dog injured in the street

once you sent me a message from a Beirut summer
a slice of Palestine's struggle
an encounter with the wrath of the froth of the sea
when darkness went thicker
than the congelations of a bad heart
the blood curdling everywhere
at the rumble and the growl
and the roar and the shriek of the heavens
being rent, rerent, and rent again
by shapes invisible born of no sane mind
and the wings of the sky
flapping death and raining sorrow
harbingers of more horror and greater sorrow
and you! You were there teaching as usual

yet beneath the infernal wrath
and in spite of it
on the boughs there, birds never ceased
to chant or pray or sing or simply chat
and further down on the hard ground
the children went on with their business of life
romping about as usual
and laughing off the demonic sky
how we could hear them
within the *Viracocha* night
each calling to each in crystal voices
children of life
bent to penetrate back into the world of light
and you brother! You were there learning

now you are back to your spring
your natural right supplants their artificial law
back in the month of May
the month of your exile
to rest by your boyhood brother in true peace
wrapped in the scent of Yafa's orange blossom
in your pre-*Viracocha* dreams
lulled by the waves
your childhood playmates

it is hard brother
to come to terms with your absence
hard to seek shade under a tree that is no more
to chew on a tooth that is no more
to think say of calling you on the phone
only to start with a shock
on remembering you are no more
to call for some advice
from a generous and resourceful friend
or to inquire about some fact or news item
and from there to wander perhaps
into something humourous or anecdotal
or even silly –

ah but this is not the time to mourn or grieve
the *Viracochas* are swarming at the door
still swinging now half open now half shut
but it is the time to pledge that we
your numerous disciples
each armed with a slice of your invincible spirit
pledge to keep our covenant
to man the door
oust the intruder
and keep the house clean and free.

When the Assault was Intended to Lydda

July 1948

Um Ramadan is dead now
long dead perhaps
but not in the living consciousness,
when barely more than a hulk of bones
she stood before her door and faced the east
that summer morning in contemplation

Ramadan was needlessly poised on the edge of town,
chatting in crow, the black birds
had penetrated the town's airspace,
Um Ramadan's chickens clucked
as they scattered about in the heat
each certain the world was his and his alone
with sense of neither fear nor faith
and she crooning as if in trance
more to the sun than to her chicks
an old rose cowering under the blazing hills.

Her thought was startled into subdued sounds,
slivers of a voice which once
had frightened the block into trembling
with the chatter of an indignant squirrel,
or burst the block's sides with laughter,
voice that now slivered
into plaintive strains of a bassoon
drained of its native humour.

The wind bore fresh chicken leavings
and traces of burnings
of olive leaves from yesterday's bakers
but the henna which scented the hair of brides
and graced their hands with its purple blood
which graced and scented them again
after the final bath
before passing into another way of being
blushed and henceforth was to go unused.

Still she faced the sun like a plant
she sniffed the decomposed days down the road
she saw the hackings of live limbs
and their scatterings so that they might forfeit their birthright
she heard, compressing links of cause and particular,
the rattle of dry blood down countless generations
she seemed to have stars for food,
and when she had her fill
she came back to chick and low-pitched crow,
back to the great 'Emathian Conqueror' poised to strike
she was her brittle hulk of bones again.

A Slice of Palestine

A human slice so massive,
it had its special gravity
suddenly cut loose from place and history
as we drifted and he still in the centre
to hold us together in orbit;

he kept his head up
when so many were falling about him;
neither the enemy's fire
nor the heat of the sun when enraged
could melt either his fat or his tough skin.

But he had not the humour to strike roots
in new times and strange places;
he had much weight;
instead he ruminated
with fire burning inward

with an appetite that turned upon itself
as we splintered out of sphere and took in the new air:
that melted him fast
a candle on a blind road,
the camel of his tribe.

Ali of Lydda

Before the conqueror shot him dead
from the top of our roof,
Ali had on his head,
as he walked homeward in the morning sun,
a tray made of straw, of circles,
none vicious though:
Each circle flowed into the next
from small to large to larger rounds:

The first bore the transformation
of the dream of wheat, its ears still close to the ground,
into loaves of exciting breath;
the second of a humble communion
of young and old breaking bread into lasting bond
under the sanctity of one roof;
the third of modest hopes
which rose and tossed like one vast field shedding green
in the wind and the ripening sun;
the fourth of a dream beyond,
half formed, half grasped –

After he shot Ali dead,
and the tray fell in manner undignified
and the bread tumbled and scattered on hot, hard stone
in shapes of heads rolling about a sanctuary,
I heard the conqueror on the high roof
under the naked sky,
I heard him snort,
I heard him clear his throat,
I heard him spit on the ground,
I heard him piss
through the eye of light.

Mother and Son

It was when and where knew neither end nor beginning,
when the moon was dazzled and the sun dazed,
when the first drop of stream's end
moved at the height of its fall,
up and down, up and down
it was then
that I came upon them:

'Just give her a little to drink.'
I handed her the jug,
but she had only a sip;
I offered him,
but he shook his head in the dazzling dark,
and they proceeded
mother and son
toward the bright midst of things,
she who was an example...
ah, an example of what...
where thirst no longer knew bounds,
and he whom I had taken
for a leaf gone dry before its time

that was when tears went frozen
for all the beating of the heart,
for then only night could see and speak.

The Bite, or the Power of Symbiosis

The beasts of the West bit them with unusual rage
and drove them yet deeper into their apartness,
beasts of dogma
beasts of creed
beasts of profit
beasts of race at its beastliest
ranging over Europe and Europe's spawn.

Like a mother who, gone mad, bites her child,
they bit them with fever-driven teeth
lusting as if after some divine blood,
then loosed them with rabid sympathy;
and they charged as if from an age
long-abandoned,
long-forgotten
from the deep recesses of the shades,
or from a future whose frenzied dark
is yet undiscovered to man,
howling infected psalms!
They charge,
those who are genuinely ill,
and those who are just ill enough to feign illness,
refining it to perfection,
so that it is hard to tell art from nature.

Foaming at the mouth they charge,
charge with fangs borrowed and fangs home-bred
bared as they rave
to tear, to sink deep, to unnerve –
disciples, through art and ardour
eclipsing their teachers!

Divinity must have erred,
even... oh no, no!
To sin is only human.

In their bite are compressed
man's sorriest diseases:
the West bit them hard and long,
hard and long,
then sicced them upon us!
Vulgarity is the mother of obscenity;

may the heavens then have pity!
Pity on those who lay no claim
to divinity or differentness of blood!
May the Almighty give us courage,
and save us from the clutches of apartness!
May the Almighty and the mighty will to live
grant us immunity
against the foam at the mouth
against the bite that is sick
and the bite of design,
against the symbiosis between teacher and disciple,
between parent and child!

Miracle of the Turkey

They left their senses without
when they entered the house
like a horde of holy men
who take off their shoes
before they enter a shrine.

With studied rage they slit the throats of twelve;
resistance was offered in scuffles and pleadings
mingled with gasps and deep red snorts
as if before an altar.

But for the flashlights,
you would have taken the event
for a heap of lovers at rough play
transgressing the bounds of a pastoral prospect

The deed done, they left
with recovered senses to their barracks –
stars retiring for the night
confident of another:
but the thirteenth!
Ah, the thirteenth! That was the wonder of wonders.

He did not hide,
there was no place to hide in the flashing of blades;
tongue-tied he could not plead
yet...and finding him still alive,
words of gratitude glittered on his tongue
like pearls on a golden thread
gushed in song, and prayer up towards Him
who kept watch over him alone
alone marked him in his mysterious way
so that he felt a pillar
standing above the ruins,
the lonely shepherd among the corpses of his tribe,

a turkey pardoned by the president,
chosen from among millions for grace,
chosen to tower in the scheme of creation,
to praise and sing the tale to dead ears –
the miracle of grace and disgrace
of image and original.

Abu Talab

It went on for nearly three decades
year after year
day after day:
He communed with none,
with neither sun nor moon,
he only roamed the narrow streets winding or straight,
he wandered among cherry orchards and through wheat fields,
now as it seemed in dialogue with himself,
now in argument
the voice rising a little,
the body constantly dwindling,
the bones ever-pushing outward
wherein the restless spirit was trapped;
the children were afraid,
and when they grew up prayed—
it was said his daughter gave her husband
all she could call her own
and then was returned to her folks
with nothing to call her own,
and a ghost roamed alley and street
as he muttered away,
the foam sometimes flowering from his mouth
he roamed and muttered, heedless of all,
of the curfew newly restored,
and his Israeli killer
may have muttered to himself
that at least he shot him out of his misery.

On the Range

The brief biography of a chicken

He was hatched on the range
to a woman, as usual old and poor
who treated him as a child of her own,
and in return he made his pledge and kept it:
He kept her company
and faithfully provided for her
by fathering numberless chicks;
this brought her much relief and comfort;

he had a curious habit which spread
a sense of security and reassurance
all over the neighbourhood and beyond;
it was his voice ranged way beyond his size,
the winds thrilled to carry it everywhere,
through branch and leaf and flower,
through every ear of wheat;

with his voice he out-called the calls to prayer
from dawn to dusk and dusk to dawn;
he out-belled the sweetest bells
be they joyful or in mourning;
he even out-horned the ram's horn
so piercing and so keen;
and every night at ten his pleading call
made the woman who had left her home for her parents',
he made her go back to her husband's
whatever hardship might still be awaiting her;
how did the members of his large family
regard him? With great awe and greater love!

The voice knit them up into a wholesome whole,
into an orbit of sacred gravity;

and so it went,
until They arrived and settled to claim all,
land and home,
short range and long range:
Dismemberment plagued the land,
they did not like the bird,
he was an intruder
come truly out of this world with the haunting calls,
it disturbed them beyond measure,
they denounced him as alien
alien in voice, in accent, and in tone!
They did not know how to silence him;
but since they had more trust in their law
than in the bird's lawlessness,
they rushed to court,
the robed man was not slow:

mysteriously the old woman was no more,
and her provider delivered to the newcomers
who celebrated that Friday evening
with a noise of their own,
for a dinner prefaced by chicken soup

and yet the echo persists,
plaintive but trumpet-clear,
it vibrates through every limb of the body,
it is heard through the soul
and haunts the holy range, ever-calling,
ever-reminding us of the covenant and the pledge.

Over the Well

He came after the fields,
after the house and its contents,
he camped near the well with whose water
I quench my thirst
and cleanse myself before I meet my maker,

he drew circles around the well and called it his,
I protested,
he looked askance and went on with his claim
that I may roam an unwashed limb under grey skies,
a brown husk in thirsty wastes;

he settled and dug in,
he dug deep beneath the flow of the waters
and took possession of the veins
so that my well paled and cowered.

Over the well there was a long and savage strife
with bruises thick and scars indelible,
and when he saw he had to leave the well
why, he pissed in it, my well,
and sulked away proclaiming to the civilized world
in the world's most civil tongue
'*Cet animal est très méchant,*
quand on l'attaque, il se défend!'

But he is gone
and I am free despite the beastliness,
all is well
save perhaps for a slight deviation,
a dream now and then of dark waters
gushing out of deep winding caves,
a bit unsettling now and then;

but I am free
free of all fear and malice,
and I remain the owner and the keeper of my well
save for a slight change:

Whenever I take a drink
I am in doubt about the taste,
whenever I limp before my Lord
I cringe a bit
I pray I do not smell.

Tell Them

Tell them there is ten thousand dollars
for him or her who wins,
and ten million shall rise and dash for it
with the passion of bulls roused to some serious business,
their dreams at loggerheads
crushing the sides and insides of the night:
greed bulges and bursts them out of sleep.

Tell them there is possible death for him or her
if hit by the one remaining bullet
and all shall uproot like dead plants from the soil,
their hearts sinking deep in their stomachs
their panting feet in tangles
as they melt away with panic
that others may fill their place.

Remembering after Forty Years in the Wilderness

Over Europe there hung a strange mist,
America was still feigning innocence,
and God was ordering that there be light

and when there was
there was paraded on the road to Ni'leen
as the wind played possum
a pair of dead breasts
and a baby his face buried between them
waiting to be nursed

the July sun was pitiless then
citing and reciting the incident when God that spring
went merciful and ordered that there be light

and when there was
there was paraded from Deir Yaseen
in the breath of the orange blossom
in the view of God's City
a baby lying on his tummy
dead between two breasts that yearned to nurse.

To Whom

To you,
beast of might even of majesty,
of loyalty and true faith
when they came in stealth to you,
chained for no known cause or need,
to club and club and club over the head
right to the unworthy end,
and you writhing with Spartan patience
uttering sounds scarcely audible,
you so pathetically ignorant
of the gifts conferred upon you –
all in the pitch of the indifferent dark?

Or to you,
child yet of slight experience
and of less consequence,
thrown down on the cold floor
with bare feet held tight
so that lash, lash, lash would go the thick stick
until the blood in protest rushes
hot and red out of the swollen feet
all for forgetting the holy book of God,
you naughty, lazy boy –
all yet in the gloom
which precedes blossom and bloom?

Or to you,
the ultimate of grace and beauty,
image of your divine maker,
flower of dignity forced down on your back,
the two gallants clutching your limbs
that the third may thrust and thrust and thrust,
his AK-47 waiting impatiently by his side
to probe through petals already torn and rent,
you on whom too much wealth has been forced
too much to understand, to bear and guard,
too much bliss not to turn into curse –
all through the bright light of day?

To who else?

In Principio Erat Verbum

My friend parades to the world his large wealth,
and he parades to the world the might
of his tongue with which he guards his wealth.
I stalk him until he notices me;

We exchange glances,
his are hostile,
I say, 'I am worried,'
and the world is worried on my behalf;

my friend and I bandy words,
his are menacing,
I say, 'I am afraid of him,'
and the world is afraid for me,

so that I give him a shove
just to find out where things stand you know,
he curses me extravagantly,
I do not answer back;

but the world warns me of the danger I am in
so that I give him such a blow
as makes fly and fall to the ground
many of his precious teeth;

the world is awed, fascinated
'But I want peace!' I cry,
he roars,
he rails loud and raves louder,

he swears, his speech deformed now like his mouth,
he swears to get me yet:
to do to me what none has dared to do
'My very existence is in grave jeopardy,'

I solemnly declare
and the world is in full sympathy
brazen and unabashed, still
he bellows vows to get me yet –
enough to finish him off
to deal him an existential blow,
and I have known all along,
contrary to the others,

that he was nothing but an empty skin
nothing but a toothless rage –
and yet I never thought the brute had so much wealth
nor so much blood!

Lullaby for an Ass

The groundhog came out this morning,
he saw his shadow
and went back for six more weeks,
went back into his solitary confinement,
so lullaby sweet baby
lullaby and good night.

Six more weeks of hibernation,
to the death of Jesus
among the apricot and cherry blossoms,
so patience my sweet one
patience until good times arrive.

No sun setting in the east shall disturb you
no mule conceiving shall resurrect you,
die then my sugar baby die
die until winter comes again
for the rebirth of your lord and brother,
succor will then be at hand.

And you shall live, my patient one
as soon as the moon shines bright at noon for you,
and the Dead Sea bears blossoms for you,
and you shall have your fill of hay at last
my sweetest ass
as soon as the chosen one,
essence of God's creation
intercedes and dies
only for you.

V

A Conversation

Bernard Gordon,
born Chicago, USA,
killed inside a Palestinian refugee camp.
Gordon was attempting to break up a demonstration
in defiance of an Israeli-imposed curfew:
How come you are in my orchard?
It was dark and I lost my way;

David Milton Green,
born Melbourne, Australia,
shot by an Arab later captured;
David was chasing into a mosque
a youth waving the Palestinian flag:
How did you get on top of my cherry tree?
It was the wolf chased and howled me up there;

Cynthia S. Isaacs,
born Odessa, Russia,
murdered with a sharp rock
in an Arab schoolyard while on police duty,
assailant still at large:
How is it there are no cherries left on the branches?
The fierce wind shook them down;

I. Dov Abromowitz,
thirty, whose grandparents perished at Auschwitz
was stabbed to death in the bedroom
of a Palestinian home
while searching for terrorist literature:
How come no cherries on the ground and your basket cherry-full?
Hell, can't you figure it out for yourself?

Fable of the Deer and the Hound

'I have panted after you,'
said the hunting dog as he pursued the deer,
'I have panted after you
beyond the length of a summer day,
beyond the length of a winter night,
but the faster and the longer I run,
the farther away you grow from me,
and I am a gifted hound
with a diploma in hunting,
while you are nothing but a deer!
Now how is that,
just tell me how is that?'
Breathless the deer replied,
'Why, that is not hard to tell,
you run for your master,
I run for myself.'

'I have fought you for a hundred years,'
said invader to defender,
'I have fought you with every means at my disposal,
with the carrot when you stiffened,
with the stick when you looked brittle,
I have killed you for the love of my God,
and I have killed you with the wrath of my God,
and yet the more I gain, the more I lose!
The more I kill you, the more you are alive!

Now how is that! Just tell me how is that?'
breathless the defender shot back:
'Why, it is hard for you to understand,
but you fight fired by the fearful appetite
for growing ever so fatter,
I fight fueled by the fear of ceasing to be.'

The Shunnar and the Olive Tree

The strength of his limbs,
not the strength of his will,
failed him at last.
The bullet had torn through his organs.
Exhausted, he sat on the rock in the afternoon sun
which was nursing the grape vines nearby
in the scent of ripe wheat and ripening olive,
his gun now lying idle beside him.
His companions had to leave hurriedly,
they had no time;
and his bride was waiting for him
to tell him the good tidings,

as he sat on the rock waiting for the other men,
men of the enemy that summer afternoon.
His limbs were failing rapidly
as the sun was failing,
his impatience beckoning
until the enemy arrived.
His comrades had headed east
and he lead or mislead the enemy west.

He needed no Spartan to teach him
cunning and steadfastness;
his teacher was his comrade the *shunnar*
who engages the intruder
with her flutter of wing and magnetic song
while her babies seek shelter
behind the sympathetic rocks
no larger than an olive or a date
or the bullet that had gunned through him.

His will moved his feet on the rugged path
until the blood ran out
like the blood of the sun as he collapsed
in the arms of the olive tree
never leafless
forever leaving,
coeval with time
with yesterday with today and with the morrow.
It was planted by those who died
for those who are living;
it is planted by those who are living
for those who will be born.

His limbs died early.
They were confined to the state of the flesh,
to a particular individual
whose life is quick to fail and pass on.
His will lives;
it is a part of the collective will, the people's will,
more long-lived than the olive.
More persistent and cunning than the *shunnar*.
That late afternoon he had delivered

like his bride who was to deliver
at early dawn that night.
Nobody attended her.
England's brave men made sure of that,
except for the three *shunnars* outside
ululating as the new life was being born.
She was up and about that morning;
there was no time to waste.
She broke her fast
for the sake of the new life
with the blood of the olive
and the flesh of wheat.

Angel at the Gate

The angel at the gate examines the ID cards,
he looks up, and at the sight
his hands cover his face
involuntarily;

But he denies admission to both,
to the one who still wobbles when he walks,
and to the other who is not yet done crawling
'In heaven,' pointing to the toddler,
still shivering as if in the jaws of a pincer of ice,
'In heaven floods are banned!
Fire too is forbidden here,'
pointing to the infant
whose flesh is dangling loose,
peeling off like a slither of feeling
as it peels off a thought or act.

'Now you both go back to where you came from,
go and tell your people that useless is the tooth abscessed at the root!
That fruitless are your baptisms
since they are tainted at conception,
tell them that fire will yet have fire,
and water, water!

And tell them, too, that here in heaven
there is no room
for either tales of Shoah or tales of Noah.'

Gallows Land

Sitti al-Hajjeh,
she was Um Omar in her younger days,
she is still poor and now all alone,
except for an elderly cat.
The sun is in his last decade
and she is on the threshold of the night.
With the few teeth still in her mouth,
she is chewing gingerly
on bread drained of much of its sap

softened by fresh tomatoes
animated by salt from the Dead Sea she believes:
They quicken the buds and palate of the hour;
and dreamily she chews in the ripe sunset.
She ruminates:
The years were young then when her man
left for the mountains with his hungry rifle
leaving her with the three little ones
arguing with one another that night

over what young Ata should order
for his last meal before his hanging,
his becoming a martyr at dawn:
'Roast chicken,
it tastes good,'
argued the eldest;
'Stuffed grape leaves,
they are yummy,'
asserted the middle one;

The youngest –
in those salad days they hanged
with heads on fire and hearts on ice.
The hangmen issued from Gallows Land,
they roamed far and wide
bearing their gallows on their backs
setting them up in every land;
they hanged before the prime
at the prime

and well after the prime.
Ah, but not before serving them on that fatal evening
the dinner of their desire;
they hanged before the crowing of the cock
before the thawing of the dew –
yes, the youngest,
he looked about him
and in a voice low and firm,
'I would feast on the flesh and blood of an Englishman.'

Not in Vain

There is no such thing the year around as easeful death,
not even in the bosom of the olive tree
when she has just risen from her green rest to bear:

Who does not writhe at the stings of thirst
at that sharp moment between the two worlds
of what is and what is not?

What earth does not shudder at the feel of young blood,
what playmates do not shiver at the sight,
what mother or sister does not weep in the dead of night?

They have died on the brow of winter:
Down their throats they rammed the bitter fruit
before their lips could touch the blossoms of birth.

They have crammed youth into the grave,
down the throat of night, at the benighted hour
which yet ignites the fire of day.

They have died to herald the birth of the Father,
therefore for all its unnaturalness
their death shall not be in vain:

They may sleep longer than their Father,
but they shall arise with Him
with the multitude of all time and colour;

Hell shall then be harrowed,
the prisons' gates flung open,
and the prisons' captives set free:

They shall spring to clear the roads and hallow them
all the way to Yafa and Haifa
to crash at the gates of God's City a load of life.

The Wife of Awad

You were young then
when the plains swarmed with the comers ashore
and the mountains thundered with fire
when the air rained gloom and defiance
and the skies flashed and screamed death from Europe;

you were young then
when the caves gurgled with plans and rumors,
and he after an endless absence
would come to steal an hour
in the warmth of your smile and the coils of your arms
in your ever-fresh bosom
his eyes would only half-close,
your lips and his saying less than your eyes,
and the leaves ringed you in their loud whisperings;

then he would leave reluctant but renewed
for another phase of blood and fire
for another dodge of the wolf
under the mutterings of the wintry wire
for another foil of the jackal
through the leaves that fell dead
and the branches that wailed bare,
and still whenever he could
he came back for renewal
whether they were spoiling the year's yield
or pre-empting its beginnings;

and you gave him all then
the dreams of your girlhood
and the fruits of your womb
and you left bare your neck and earlobes
your fingers and your arms
bare that he might return fire with fire;

and so it went
away from you
and back to you
until like his two younger brothers before him
he met his death when day was being born
and left you with a bunch of chicks to rock and feed;

you are old now,
white is your hair
bent your figure
yet rising is the fury of the camps
and ablaze the mountains
and the odour of Treblinka's fumes mingles with the blood;

you are old now and your grandchildren have multiplied,
like your young man before them
they dodge and foil
in their fearless eyes and supple hands
they carry the seeds of eternity
they come gasping into your broad thin smile
the sweat of grownups on their brows
the tears running down their childish faces
and the hearts ticking
in the rhythm of gun and sledgehammer;

they nestle into the curvings of your bare chest
and you still heal their broken limbs
and restore the power of flight to their wings
you embrace them with the oldest fire
you kiss into their spirits its fever
and before they surge forth you give them all,
a stone,
a stone bursting with the pitiless tide
in the petals of a host of spring flowers,
it overwhelms a swarm
that has sunk from ill to mad:

ah, you mind-baffling tree
ever younger than your green
as old as the land of your roots,
you priestess of peace and witch of war,
your shriveled lips loosen the grip of death
like the lips of eternal youth,
your wrinkled breasts nurse and sustain
the plenty of unending summer.

In Memory of Ismail Shammout

I

In its craft the brook winds as it babbles
babbles as it winds
into the stream which widens as it runs,
rushes and swells as it widens
into the open sea
the all enfolding all containing sea:
they all feed from the pulse
of the fountain of all;

In its craft the first is the round of beauty
still as heaven conceived it,
it winds naturally into the widening round
of art which feeds the flow and feeds upon the flow
into the third round of life ever widening
ever expanding like the wings of the olive bearing dove:
they all drink from the fountain
of all, and they flourish.

II

You were quiet among us on the beach
when we were as boisterous as the waves
and ate the fish without ceremony,
your eyes dreaming beyond us, beyond the waves,
we played barefoot on the concrete
which the summer sun had set on fire,
we railed and we swore
while your eye held speech with the eye of the sun,

and when we sought the golden cactus fruit
still half in sleep and half in wakefulness,
you watched the skies for signs,
you seemed to have a vision of a new dawn –
you were quiet then, so quiet we thought
you counted words a crime and sound a sin
until they hurt you, bit you into the fever
which fueled and moved you through your years.

III

It moved you into a rage of creation
which challenged, without rancor
but with faith the primacy of the word,
conception in the brain
design by the eye
and touch of hand,
and there a soundless tale as simple and as cunning as that:
bring them all together

place them side by side
with your cunning and ruthless art:
the sun bearing children and the frigid dark
the olive tree and the saw in false fever
children at play in clusters and the artful cluster bomb
the water of the brook and the water heavy with pain and sorrow
the flow of milk and the flow of blood
increase endless and the dead end of the circular.

IV

Yes, place them all side by side,
with the magic of your craft
yoke them each to each into your lofty edifice:
children are on the increase
motherhood ever prevalent
the old man with his staff
shall yet charm the stone wall into a wall of children
and those wandering in exile shall return.

Now the day is winding down,
the eye of the sun narrowing down
too late though for the forces of the dark:
already your fever has caught so many
and Ismail runs in the general stream
in the blood circulation of the people,
countless are they who bear your fire,
so may you rest in peace in the prayer of the olive and the dove.

Dialogue between Lambs and Saxophones

At the spring
we drank the virgin water
straight from cups
fashioned out of children's palms;

that was in a remote land
at a time at an age
even more remote
from the eloquence of fat saxophones

where we now swing
tirelessly
circuitously
from champagne in paper cups

to Coke in crystal glasses,
unlike when we swung
simply on clothes lines
to the bleating of lean lambs.

Journey of a Curse

With a screeching twang
the angry arrow parted from the bow
and pushed the day toward an early end,
and, competing with the speed of light,
the keen heart of darkness pierced the heart of light,
and all the gods shed bitter tears,
and on Hoedr, slayer of Baldr, his brother,
was laid a curse to the end of time,
and twilight came to have a say in our things.

Well down the road,
the afternoon had all but withdrawn,
when the child drew wide apart his slingshot,
offspring of some old prophet:
The rock sped singing,
and stopped the melody of the shepherd's flute,
down in the valley already darkening;
the shepherd was old,
he panted up the hill,
he paused at what he saw,
he cursed under his breath:
'No wonder God smote you blind!'
He spat on his left,
his footsteps echoed into the dusk.

II

Tired of carrying the curse upon his back,
the child walked outside into the silence,
into that holiest of nights,
he listened until the gates of heaven
opened wide its gates,
And down upon his knees went he
with palms upturned,
he prayed,
he prayed that God give him back his eyes
that he might be like all the boys,
he went inside and waited through the night,
but day brought back no sight;

III

And as the Holy City bled red and dark,
the man of piety,
Father of his people
who was to travel far in search of succor against an inveterate oppressor,
blessed the child without sight,
and prayed him to bless the pious man:
How can he say a blessing or be blessed
puzzled the curse-bearing child?

But then the Gods for some reason
which human reason cannot fathom
took away the sight of Demodocus
only to give him such inner sight
as would make him sing
the sweetest songs in which he told the sweetest tales

IV

And it was upon a sunny morning,
not yet far into the year,
when the blind child,
now on the threshold of seeing,
recited to a couple in the prime of life:

'When man is good,
he is higher than the angels;
when he is not good,
he is lower than the beasts.'
The couple listened with wonder and humility,
'God blessed the blind for reasons
man's ken may never probe!'

Notes

The Wedding
The children's skipping rhyme means: 'I am the beloved dark one, / my wedding place is in the cup, / I wear cardamom for perfume, / my fame reaches into faraway China.'

Dafoura
Dafoura is the precursor of the fig fruit.

Trial at Ramleh
Ramleh is a Palestine town ten miles east of the port of Yafa on the Mediterranean.

Peaches
The blind child is the author.

Progress of the Sun
The story in the first stanza is told by the pharmacist in Lydda.

Boasting
This poem is based on a Palestinian saying.

The Orphan
The woman is the poet's mother.

By the Sacred Cave
Abu Huraira is the diminutive of *cat* in Arabic.

Bilal
Bilal was the first black Muslim. The Prophet appointed him his muezzin to call the Muslims to prayer.

The Palm Tree
In the Qur'an's telling of the birth of Jesus, Mary is instructed to shake the date tree.

The Pity of it
Abu al-'Ala' al-Ma'arri (973–1057) was a celebrated blind Arab poet and philosopher.

Eve
Here the stories of Abraham and his father, and Noah and his son are based on the versions in the Qu'ran.

For Now
Immisliman and Prophet's Mare are insects.

In Exile
Based on a real woman who lived in Jerusalem.

The Betrayal of Joseph
Based on an incident at Al-Nabi Rubin, south of Yafa.

Dead End
This poem compares trees in an Israeli forest with Lydda's olive trees; the decorative versus the practical.

After the Long March
Mutih was my classmate in high school. He came from the village of al-Muzairiah where he was killed at dawn when the Israelis stormed the village in 1948.

At Sitti's
The incident takes place at Al-Kuttab, a one-room school for children. Sitti is a sort of title used to address an older lady, literally 'grandma.'

Awad
Awad was a Palestinian fighter during the 1936 Rebellion. Very little is known about him except that, like hundreds of Palestinian fighters, he was hanged by the British. This poem is said to have been composed by him on the night before his execution, and was found etched on the wall of his cell.

The Beam
Farhan al-Sa'di, of the village of al-Mazar near Jineen, Palestine, was hanged by the British at the age of eighty, during the month of Ramadan, on 27 November 1937, on the charge of possessing a weapon (it was a rusted relic from the time of Ottoman rule).

Manning the Door
'When the Indians saw the very great cruelties which the Spaniards committed everywhere on entering Peru, not only would they never believe us to be Christians and children of God, as boasted, but not even that we were born on this earth, or generated by a man and born of a woman; so fierce an animal they concluded must be the offspring of the sea, and therefore called us *Viracochas*, for in their language they call the sea *cocha* and the froth *vira*; thus they think that we are a congelation of the sea, and have been nourished by the froth; and that we are come to destroy the world... They say that the winds ruin houses and break down trees, and the fire burns them; but the *Viracochas* devour everything, they consume the very earth, they force the rivers... they make war, they kill each other, they rob, they swear, they are renegades, they never speak the truth, and they deprive us of our support. Finally the Indians curse the sea for having cast such very wicked and harsh beings on the land.' (G. Benzoni, quoted in *The Golden Bough*.)

When the Assault Was Intended to Lydda
The Israelis attacked the village from the Jewish settlement of Ben Shemen, East of Lydda. Ramadan was the name of the woman's son. It is also the month of fasting for Muslims during which Lydda was conquered by the Israelis and its people forcibly driven out. 'Emathian Conqueror' is Alexander the Great; the phrase is borrowed from John Milton.

A Slice of Palestine
Based on a real figure, Haj Sa'id al-Hnaidi. Haj Sa'id was quite heavy.

Ali of Lydda
Lydda is a Palestinian town about ten miles east of Yafa.

Mother and Son
For the story of carrying a little water to a friend's mother during the forced march from Lydda see *In the Land of My Birth: A Palestinian Boyhood.*

Abu Talab
Abu Talab was from Hebron. He went mad after his daughter was divorced and returned to him; one day he was shot dead by the Israelis for violating the curfew.

Remembering after Forty Years in the Wilderness
Ni'leen is a Palestinian village to which 60,000 Palestinians were marched by the Israelis from Lydda in July 1948. Deir Yaseen is the village where the Irgun, led by Menachem Begin, massacred hundreds of Palestinians in April of that year.

Lullaby for an Ass
There is a Palestinian saying, 'Die, ass, stay dead until the hay comes.'

The Shunnar and the Olive Tree
'An Arab gangster who, after firing at the troops, acted as guide and took them to a neighbouring village, collapsed and died of a bullet wound after walking two kilometers with them. The incident happened last Wednesday near Ataroth (Atara). After firing at a band of snipers the military patrol found an Arab villager sitting on a boulder. He had thrown away his rifle. He said he came from a neighbouring village. The troops ordered him to lead them there to verify his assertion. The man led them over stony mountain paths for two kilometers. Suddenly he collapsed and died. Upon being examined, they found that he had been shot clear through the stomach, and the bullet had come out through his back.' (*The Palestine Post* 10 August 1936.)

Not in Vain
Yafa and Haifa are two Palestinian coastal cities seized by the Israelis and depopulated of their Arab inhabitants in 1948.

In Memory of Ismail Shammout
Ismail Shammout (1930-2006) was Palestinian artist and art historian known all over the Arab world and beyond. Born in Lydda, his most famous painting *Where to ..?* (1953) depicts the Lydda death march in 1948. He and the author were boyhood friends.

Journey of a Curse
The man of piety is Haj Amin Al-Husaini. In Nordic mythology Heodr is a blind god who accidentally kills his twin brother Baldr, the god of light.

Acknowledgements

Thanks are due to the editors of the following publications where some of these poems were first published – *Anemone, Arab Studies Quarterly, Confluence, Ellipsis, Indiannual, In Print, Interim, International Poetry Review, Mind in Motion, The New Renaissance, North Atlantic Review, Onionhead, Orbis, Pig Iron, The Plowman, Profile of a Poet, Sombra, The Sow's Ear, Trestle Creek Review, Voices International*; Reja-e Busailah, *We Are Human Too: Poems on the Palestinian Condition* (1985), Ahmad H. Sa'di and Lila Abu-Lughod (eds), *Nakba: Palestine, 1948, and the Claims of Memory* (2007), Grace Beeler, Joan Dobbie and Edward Morin (eds) *Before There is Nowhere to Stand: Palestine/Israel, Poets Respond to the Struggle* (2012).